AF605179

In Your 50s

In Your 50s has been created by writer and researcher Judy Valon and renowned artist and designer Roger Roberts, whose illustrations featured in the hugely successful Toddler Taming books. Coincidentally both born in Wales, UK, Judy and Roger now live in Adelaide, South Australia. Together they have created a series of stylish, fun and covetable gift books for the global market.

In Your 50s

Author Judy Valon Illustrator Roger Roberts

Wakefield Press
1 The Parade West
Kent Town
South Australia 5067
www.wakefieldpress.com.au

First published 2009

Designed by Judy Valon and Roger Roberts
Printed in China at Everbest Printing Co. Ltd

National Library of Australia Cataloguing-in-Publication entry

Author: Valon, Judy.
Title: In your 50s/Judy Valon; illustrator Roger Roberts.
ISBN: 978 1 86254 820 6 (hbk.).
Subjects:
Middle age – Quotations, maxims, etc.
Middle age – Humor.
Aging – Quotations, maxims, etc.
Aging – Humor.
Other Authors/Contributors: Roberts, Roger, 1943– .
Dewey Number: 305.2440207

So, now you are fifty. You've survived the interesting years between forty and fifty, and all that they bring, and you're ready to take on the next decade. Take heed, apply the right attitude, assume a positive outlook, and the next decade could bring some of the best years of your life. You are established, you have settled down, and your sense of self is strong. You might be fifty but inside you still feel twenty-one. Make the most of every day and every situation – reinvigorate your life, take up a new hobby, plant a vegetable garden, get fit, change your career – the sky's the limit. Here's to happiness, good health and life lived to the fullest.

The process of maturing is an art to be learned, an effort to be sustained. By the age of fifty you have made yourself what you are, and if it is good, it is better than your youth

Marya Mannes

All that I know I learned after I was thirty

Georges Clemenceau

Live your life and forget your age

Norman Vincent Peale

Old age is like everything else – to make a success of it you have to start young

Fred Astaire

Middle age is when work is a lot more fun and fun is a lot more work

Unknown

To keep the heart unwrinkled, to be hopeful, kindly, cheerful, reverent – that is to triumph over old age

Thomas Bailey Aldrich

Today the world changes so quickly that in growing up we take leave not just of youth but of the world we were young in

Peter Medawar

In three words I can sum up everything I've learned about life: 'it goes on'

Robert Frost

Middle age is the time when a man is always thinking that in a week or two he will feel as good as ever

Don Marquis

Middle age is youth without levity, and age without decay

Doris Day

The older I grow the more I distrust the familiar doctrine that age brings wisdom

H.L. Mencken

Nature gives you the face you have at twenty; it is up to you to merit the face you have at fifty

Coco Chanel

When I was younger, I could remember anything, whether it had happened or not; but my faculties are decaying now and soon I shall be so I cannot remember any but the things that never happened. It is sad to go to pieces like this but we all have to do it

Mark Twain

Age merely shows what children we remain

Johann Wolfgang von Goethe

Experience is the one thing that you get for nothing

Oscar Wilde

I think I've discovered the secret of life – you just hang around until you get used to it

Charles M. Schulz

Maturity is only a short break in adolescence

Jules Feiffer

When I was young, I thought that money was the most important thing in life; now that I am old, I know it is

Oscar Wilde

Youth is when you're allowed to stay up late on New Year's Eve. Middle age is when you're forced to

Bill Vaughan

No man is ever old enough to know better

Holbrook Jackson

Old age is like a plane flying through a storm. Once you're aboard, there's nothing you can do

Golda Meir

How old would you be if you didn't know how old you are?

Satchel Paige

It takes a long time to become young

Pablo Picasso

It is not the length of life, but depth of life

Ralph Waldo Emerson

Where have you put my glasses?

Middle age is when your age starts to show around your middle

Start every day off with a smile and get it over with

W.C. Fields

Like many women my age, I am twenty-eight years old

Mary Schmich

Laugh at yourself and always look in a full-length mirror

Funk up the glasses – get something bright and cool

When it comes to staying young, a mind-lift beats a facelift any day

Marty Bucella

Age should not have its face lifted, but rather it should teach the world to admire wrinkles as the etchings of experience and the firm line of character

Ralph B. Perry

If wrinkles must be written upon our brows, let them not be written upon the heart. The spirit should never grow old

James A. Garfield

The problem with beauty is that it's like being born rich and getting poorer

Joan Collins

You can’t turn back the clock. But you can wind it up again

Bonnie Prudden

You can’t help getting older, but you don’t have to get old

George Burns

The secret of staying young is to live honestly, eat slowly, and lie about your age

Lucille Ball

Age spots

Life is the art of drawing without an eraser

John W. Gardner

Youth is a wonderful thing. What a crime to waste it on children

George Bernard Shaw

A man is as old as he's feeling, a woman as old as she looks

Mortimer Collins

Fly me to the moon

Dress funky while you still can

Have your hair any colour you like – give up the natural highlights

You know you've reached middle age when a doctor not a policeman tells you to slow down

Unknown

All you exercise are your prerogatives and it takes you longer to rest than to get tired

Unknown

Don't look back. Something might be gaining on you

Satchel Paige

I still find each day too short for all the thoughts I want to think, all the walks I want to take, all the books I want to read and all the friends I want to see

John Burroughs

Now that I think of it I wish I had been a hellraiser when I was thirty. I tried it when I was fifty but I always got sleepy

Groucho Marx

None are so old as those who have outlived enthusiasm

Henry David Thoreau

Relish your hair, it will soon be gone!

I think men who have a pierced ear are better prepared for marriage. They've experienced pain and bought jewellery

Rita Rudner

Inflation is when you pay fifteen dollars for the ten dollar haircut you used to get for five dollars when you had hair

Sam Ewing

Middle age is when you choose your cereal for the fibre not the toy!

Go the gym, firm up the flabby bits

Alas, after a certain age every man is responsible for his face

Albert Camus

Everything slows down with age apart from the time it takes cake and ice cream to reach your hips

Attributed to John Wagner

Like a lot of fellows around here, I have a furniture problem. My chest has fallen into my drawers

Billy Casper

Now you are over fifty you should get more fresh air and exercise, so drive with the car windows open

I’ve got everything I always had only it’s six inches lower

Gypsy Rose Lee

I’m not offended by all the dumb blonde jokes because
I know I’m not dumb – and I’m also not blonde

Dolly Parton

Youth is the gift of nature, but age is a work of art

Stanislaw Lec

Have a makeover – make the beautician your new best friend

Smile more – the lines are there anyway so you may as well have fun!

In a man's middle years there is scarcely a part of the body he would hesitate to turn over to the proper authorities

E.B. White

I don't plan to grow old gracefully; I plan to have facelifts until my ears meet

Rita Rudner

What do you think of my new lips, George?

Take 10,000 steps every day

What matters most is how you see yourself

Unknown

Discover your neighbourhood and meet your neighbours

Make time to discover yourself, make new friends and visit new places

Give me golf clubs, fresh air and a beautiful partner, and you can keep the clubs and the fresh air

Jack Benny

Golf is played by twenty million mature American men whose wives think they are out having fun

Jim Bishop

As you walk down the fairway of life you must smell the roses, for you only get to play one round

Ben Hogan

Play golf

Champions keep playing until they get it right

Billie Jean King

Do you know what my favourite part of the game is?
The opportunity to play

Mike Singletary

Many men go fishing all of their lives without knowing that it is not fish they are after

Henry David Thoreau

The supreme accomplishment is to blur the line between work and play

Arnold J. Toynbee

I find that a man is as old as his work. If his work keeps him from moving forward, he will look forward with work

William Ernest Hocking

Change your career

Do you know the difference between education and experience? Education is when you read the fine print; experience is what you get when you don't

Pete Seeger

Old age is an excellent time for outrage. My goal is to say or do at least one outrageous thing every week

Louis Kronenberger

Twenty years from now you will be more disappointed by the things that you didn't do than the ones you did

Mark Twain

Learn something, take a new hobby, go back to study

Change is inevitable – except from a vending machine

Robert C. Gallagher

Things do not change; we change

Henry David Thoreau

If you're in a bad situation, don't worry it'll change.
If you're in a good situation, don't worry it'll change

John A. Simone Sr

When you are through changing, you are through

Bruce Barton

Because things are the way they are, things will not stay the way they are

Bertolt Brecht

If you don't like something, change it. If you can't change it, change your attitude. Don't complain

Maya Angelou

Challenge yourself

People grow through experience if they meet life honestly and courageously. This is how character is built

Eleanor Roosevelt

While one finds company in himself and his pursuits, he cannot feel old, no matter what his years may be

Amos Bronson Alcott

The real voyage of discovery consists not in seeking new landscapes but in having new eyes

Marcel Proust

Your greatest wealth is in your mind

Paul J. Meyer

Explore your spiritual side

I arise in the morning torn between a desire to improve the world and a desire to enjoy the world. This makes it hard to plan the day

E.B. White

By the time we've made it, we've had it!

Malcolm Forbes

The idea is to die young as late as possible

Ashley Montagu

Youth is the best time to be rich, and the best time to be poor

Euripides

Age considers; youth ventures

Rabindranath Tagore

Everything must end, meanwhile we must amuse ourselves

Voltaire

A man is as old as his arteries

Thomas Sydenham

Growing old is like being increasingly penalised for a crime you haven't committed

Anthony Powell

Growing old is no more than a bad habit which a busy person has no time to form

Andre Maurois

The first sign of maturity is to discover that the volume knob also turns to the left

Jerry M. Wright

Hardware: the parts of a computer that can be kicked

Jeff Pesis

The good news about computers is that they do what you tell them to do. The bad news about computers is that they tell you what you tell them to do

Ted Nelson

To err is human – and to blame it on a computer is even more so

Robert Orben

Never trust a computer you can't throw out a window

Steve Wozniak

The computer is a moron

Peter Druckner

Please key in your pin number
Uh Oh, I've gone blank
BIG BANK

Memory loss

You can't hide your true colours as you approach the autumn of your life

Unknown

The years between fifty and seventy are the hardest. You are always being asked to do more, and you are not yet decrepit enough to turn them down

T.S. Eliot

Life consists not in holding good cards but in playing those you hold well

Josh Billings

When you reach the heart of life you shall find beauty in all things

Kahill Gibran

Just remember once you're over the hill
you begin to pick up speed

Charles M. Schultz

As one grows older, one climbs with surprising strides

George Sand

There is more to life than increasing speed

Mohandas Ghandi

No wise man ever wished to be younger

Jonathan Swift

Age does not diminish the extreme disappointment of having a scoop of ice cream fall from the cone

Jim Feibig

Time is a dressmaker specialising in alterations

Faith Baldwin

The really frightening thing about middle age is the knowledge that you'll grow out of it

Doris Day

Life is half spent before we know what it is

George Herbert

The awareness of the ambiguity of one's highest achievements (as well as one's deepest failures) is a definite symptom of maturity

Paul Tillich

I refuse to admit I am more than fifty,
even if that does make my sons illegitimate

Lady Astor

A lifestyle is what you pay for; a life is what pays you

Thomas Leonard

Bashfulness is an ornament to youth, but a reproach to old age

Aristotle

He that will not apply new remedies must expect new evils; for time is the greatest innovator

Francis Bacon

True terror is to wake up one morning and realise that your high school class is running the country

Kurt Vonnegut

When we remember we are all mad, the mysteries disappear and life stands explained

Mark Twain

To get rich never risk your health. For it is the truth that health is the wealth of wealth

Richard Baker

Middle age is the awkward period when Father Time starts catching up with Mother Nature

Harold Coffin

Age is not a particularly interesting subject. Anyone can get old. All you have to do is live long enough

Don Marquis

In the Middle Ages, twenty-one was regarded as middle aged!

Start getting used to being invisible

Love seems the swiftest, but it is the slowest of growths.
No man or woman knows what perfect love is until they
have been married a quarter of a century

Mark Twain

Those who love deeply never grow old; they may die of old age, but they die young

Dorothy Canfield Fisher

The age of a woman doesn't mean a thing. The best tunes are played on the oldest fiddles

Ralph Waldo Emerson

Another hot flush dear?

Nice one

Hello. Is that, adventurous, single and young at heart?
Personal column

Yes'm, old friends is always best, 'less you can catch a new one that's fit to make an old one out of

Sarah Orne Jewett

In youth we are plagued by desire; in later years, by the desire to feel desire

Mignon McLaughlin

The more I live, the more I think that humour is the saving sense

Jacob August Riis

Wakefield Press is an independent publishing and
distribution company based in Adelaide, South Australia.
We love good stories and publish beautiful books.
To see our full range of titles, please visit our website at
www.wakefieldpress.com.au.